THE
LAW OF KINDS

The Law of Kinds

A Key to Good Character Development

ANTHONY ADEFARAKAN

GLOEM, CANADA

CONTENTS

~ ~
INTRODUCTION
1

~ chapter one ~
THE TREE PRINCIPLE
3

~ chapter two ~
THE FRUIT PRINCIPLE
7

~ chapter three ~
THE SEED PRINCIPLE
9

~ chapter four ~
THE LAW OF KINDS
13

~ chapter five ~
PRODUCING GOOD FRUITS
21

~ chapter six ~
REMAINING A GOOD TREE
31

~ chapter seven ~
THE DANGER OF UNFRUITFULNESS
35

~ chapter eight ~
THE DANGER OF BEARING BAD FRUITS
37

~ ~
PRAYER POINTS
41

~ ~
BECOME A FINANCIAL PARTNER WITH JESUS
43

~ ~
ABOUT THE AUTHOR
45

INTRODUCTION

In the history of mankind so far, it has never been recorded that a particular species of animal reproduced another species of animal; neither has it entered the record that a particular plant species produced a fruit which belongs to another plant species.

This has never happened and it's not about to happen simply because it can never happen. In the same way, a man will always exhibit the contents of his heart just as a mirror reflects images back to the objects. A mad man does not need any form of introduction for him to be recognized, neither does a drunk need to announce that he is drunk; no matter how he pretends, his drunken state will give him away.

This book not only analyzes the problems with fruit bearing, but also provides the ways by which the problems can be addressed right from the root. That is, not just curing the effects of leakage but blocking the leakages all together. In addition to this, it will open your eyes to the reasons behind your actions as well as the ability to possess right motives, actions and consequently attract positive reactions. It's all about **"character molding"**; and what you do as a result of the truth encountered in this book will go a long way to tell "who you really are". You will be amazed at your discovery. Let's read on.

Anthony Adefarakan.

~ CHAPTER ONE ~

THE TREE PRINCIPLE

"And out of the ground the Lord God made every tree grow that is pleasant to the sight and good for food" Genesis 2:9a (NKJV).
"He shall be like a tree…" Psalm 1:3 (NKJV).

"Living" in Trees

To live means to be alive; having life, remaining alive, to remain in existence or to survive - according to the same lexicon. A tree can be said to be living as long as it still draws life from its source which is the soil (earth). As a result, such a tree will be seen standing, blossoming, strong, healthy and full of life. All the nutrients needed for livelihood are supplied by the soil and all the tree need do is to access them for utilization through its taproot system. The reason this root is called tap root is because it goes deep down to locate the resources and then taps them, supplying them upward for the tree's consumption so as to continue living. Thus, "Living" in Trees simply means remaining connected to the source of life (without which death is inevitable).

"Growing" in Trees

Growth is all about developing, increasing in size or quantity, becoming greater, becoming mature over a period of time etc. Trees exhibit growth in various forms. We have root growth, stem growth, branch growth, flower growth, fruit growth etc. How did I know? A tree planted in 1980 and the one planted in 2000 would not have the same size or level of development by 2008. Growth occurs as days go by and as it occurs, maturity sets in - which is the quality needed to withstand the many adverse conditions the young trees are vulnerable to. However, this growth does not just occur on its own, it has to be as a result of the nutrients supplied by the soil among other factors. Thus, 'growing' in trees also means remaining connected to the source of life (without which growth is a mirage).

"Bearing" in Trees

To bear means to produce, to yield, to show forth, to bring to being etc. Trees exhibit this as well. They bear branches from the trunk and the branches in turn produce or yield flowers, leaves and fruits. No tree lacks the ability to bear; if it does not produce fruits, at least it will be able to bear leaves. "Bearing" is characteristic of all trees.

However, no tree can bear anything by its own power, it must be according to the power released by its source; the soil among other factors. Thus, "Bearing" in Trees still means remaining connected to the source of life (without which barrenness is inevitable).

Having considered these characteristics exhibited by trees, it can be inferred that the "Tree Principle" is the principle of man.

At creation, the Lord said *"... let the earth bring forth grass, the herb that yields seeds and the fruit tree that yield fruit, according to its kind, whose seed is in itself, on the earth; and it was so"*. (Genesis 1:11). And He went further to create man in His own image; male and female, and breathed into his nostrils the breath of life which made man become a living being (Genesis 1:27, 2:7). By contrast, the source or origin of trees is the earth, while the source or origin of man is God Himself. It is this breath that is sustaining life in us. So, man was created to have dominion, authority and control over all other creatures by virtue of whose breathe he carries. Man can successfully carry out the characteristics of living things taught us in Biology. He can move, respire, feed, respond to stimuli, grow, excrete and he can reproduce after his own kind. Man was also empowered to do more than these. He can create, think, build, construct, command, decree, heal, deliver, set free (liberate), bind, loose, do miracles, signs and wonders etc. However, just as a tree will never be able to do or become anything outside the life given to it by the soil - its source, man will never amount to anything or even carry out any of those functions outside the life given by his Source - which is God. John 15:5 says *"...without me, you can do nothing"*. Do you recognize God as your Source?

~ CHAPTER TWO ~

THE FRUIT PRINCIPLE

"Then God said, "Let the earth bring forth grass, the herb that yields seed, and the fruit tree that yields fruit, whose seed is in itself according to its kind ..." Genesis 1:11.

"Then God blessed them, and God said to them "Be fruitful..." Genesis 1:28.

In other words, fruits are results of individual trees' configuration. In like manner, man was created by God with the ability to bear fruits i.e. he was created like a fruit tree. And as a result, he is expected to bear fruits as long as he lives. This is also a command and not an appeal. God said - "...*Be fruitful ...*" in Gen 1:28; so it's a situation he can't help, he must bear fruit as long as he's still connected to God - his life Source. And like the fruit trees, man will always manifest varieties of fruits - wickedness, righteousness, anger, generosity, kindness, cruelty, greed, covetousness, gentleness, meekness, patience, laziness, procrastination, wastefulness, punctuality, lateness, peace, strife, envy, jealousy, violence, love etc.

These fruits are not the same, though some of them may be similar. But unlike the fruit trees, a man can produce more than a type of fruit, just that they will have to belong to the same class or category. Take for instance, wickedness, jealousy, greed, cruelty, envy, strife, anger and the likes belong to the same category while love, joy, peace, patience, meekness, gentleness, kindness, generosity and the likes belong to another category. So a man can yield more than a fruit, just that it will have to be from the same category. This is a settled matter as two fruits from different categories cannot be found at the same time in a man. Man's fruit-bearing is category based.

The fruit principle therefore is also a principle of man as both the tree and man have fruit bearing as a common factor. What category then do your fruits belong?

~ CHAPTER THREE ~

THE SEED PRINCIPLE

"Then God said, "Let the earth bring forth grass, the herb that yields fruit, whose seed is in itself according to its kind..." Genesis 1:11.

"...for whatever a man sows, that he will also reap". Galatians 6:7b.

Seeds are the parts of a plant from which new plants of the same kind grow. The parts of a plant containing the seeds are the fruits. These seeds (locked up in the fruits) are capable of regenerating themselves into the full likeness of the plants they are taken from, and this they can do not only once, but as long as they are given the opportunity to do so - i.e. whenever they are planted or sown in a "living" soil.

These seeds have some characteristics worthy of note;

1. Some are usually small (unnoticeable) when still in their inert (inactive) state.
2. They are usually unattractive; reason for the dictionary using "seedy" for things that are untidy, dirty or not respectable in appearance.
3. Although they have life in them; they must still die before they can live and yield more plants - John 12:24

4. No one can predict their ability or capability until they prove it themselves.
5. The death of a seed is the burial of a forest.
6. They always reproduce after their own kind i.e. the seed of a particular plant will not produce a different plant.
7. They have different germination periods and as such they have different periods of growth and yield i.e. two different seeds may not grow and yield at the same time. It depends on the gestation periods of individual seeds.
8. They can be killed and destroyed simply by killing and destroying the fruit that is bearing them.
9. They are what makes a fruit a fruit i.e. a fruit is so called only because it has seeds.
10. They can survive to distant generations because once they are sown, harvest is inevitable, provided the earth still remains - Genesis 8:22.

These are just to mention a few; seeds are mysterious in functions.

However, relating this to man, it is evidently clear that the fruits mentioned in the previous chapters have various seeds embedded in them. That is, the fruits in the first category have their seeds while those in the other category have theirs too. And they are very much capable of regenerating themselves into the same fruits still in their different categories. Take for instance, "wickedness" as a fruit has "wicked seeds" embedded in it, and once they are planted or sown, it becomes inevitable for them to reproduce wickedness and even in greater measure because the harvest is always greater or more than the seeds sown - just as seed of avocado would produce many avocado fruits on a single plant. The only condition that will not make a man have a bountiful harvest from his seeds is if the seeds were not planted. But once they are planted, God will naturally make sure they turn to harvest. Although it may take some time, delay is not denial. If you show favour, you will reap favour, if you show mercy, you will reap mercy, if you show hatred, you will reap hatred - all in greater measures. You can't reap what you didn't sow just as you can't reap orange by planting pawpaw. It is not possible. Thus, the seed principle is the principle of man as well. What are you sowing - in words, actions, behaviours, eating, drinking, relationships, and service to God?

Don't be deceived, your harvest will tell. Read Galatians 6:7-8, Matthew. 7:1-2, Luke 6:38; and 2 Corinthians 9:6.

~ CHAPTER FOUR ~

THE LAW OF KINDS

"Therefore, by their fruits, you will know them" - Matthew 7:20.

The Book of Genesis Chapter 1, verse 21 through 27 gives an account of the origin of this law. It reads:

"So God created great sea creatures and every living thing that moves, with which the waters abounded, according to their kind, and every winged bird according to its kind. And God saw that it was good.

And God blessed them, saying. "Be fruitful and multiply, and fill the waters in the seas, and let birds multiply on the earth"

So the evening and the morning were the fifth day.

Then God said "Let the earth bring forth the living creature according to its kind: cattle and creeping thing and beast of the earth, each according to its kind", and it was so.

And God made the beast according to its kind, cattle according to its kind, and everything that creeps on the earth according to its kind. And God saw that it was good.

Then God said, "Let us make man in our image, according to our likeness: let them have dominion over the fish of the sea, over the birds of the air, and over the cattle, over all the earth and over every creeping thing that creeps on the earth"

So God created man in His own image, in the image of God He created him; male and female, He created them."

A close observation at this passage clearly reveals the reoccurrence or repetition of a particular phrase - **"according to its kind"**. What does this really mean?

Simply put, it means: "In its likeness" i.e. "as it is", "a copy of itself" "just like it" etc. That was the order in which God created all things.

This law of kinds simply states that **"kind begets kind" and "like begets like"**.

Who originated the law? Go over the text again. God made everything according to its kind - the fish in the sea, the birds of the air, the cattle and beast of the field, the creeping things on the earth surface and even man after His own likeness (His kind).

This explains the reason a cat will always give birth to a cat and not to a rat or fish, and it also explains why a man will never reproduce pineapple fruit nor a banana tree bear melon as fruit. That is the order of God.

This law however finds full expression in our character as human beings. We tend to appear good to all men, and of course, no one wants to be seen as bad. But Luke 5:43 - 45 says:

"For a good tree does not bear bad fruit, nor does a bad tree bear good fruit. For every tree is known by its own fruit. For men do not gather figs from thorns, nor do they gather grapes from a bramble bush. A good man out of the good treasure of his heart brings forth good, and an evil man out of the evil treasure of his heart brings forth evil. For out of the abundance of the heart his mouth speaks".

What this passage is saying in essence is that a man cannot be good and bad at the same time. It's either he is a good man or he is a bad man; just as no spring can send forth fresh and bitter water from the same opening nor yield both salt water and fresh according to James 3:11-12.

Your character is your life. In fact, the Oxford Advanced Learner's Dictionary defines it as all the mental or moral qualities that make a person, group, nation etc. different from others OR all the features that make a thing, a place, an event etc what it is and different from others. Your character is "you" personified. Just as no two individuals on the surface of the earth no matter how close or blood related can have the same fingerprint, no other person can have your exact character. They may be similar, but they can never be the same. It is what makes you 'you' and not 'him' or 'her' or 'them'. This character can either be positive or negative, strong or weak, refined or raw, attractive or repulsive, winning or losing etc. In short, it always comes as "word" and "opposite" in different individuals. It can't be good and bad in a single individual.

However, one striking and fearful thing about this character is that "it is like smoke that can't be covered as it will always find expression - either voluntarily or involuntarily on your own part". For instance, Moses wore the garment of meekness to cover his in-built (occasional) anger for over 80 years, and he thought all was well. But on a particular fateful day, the anger outgrew the covering of the meekness garment and exploded (having been compressed for long) and the result was an irreversible termination of destiny.

You can read Numbers 20:7-12, Deuteronomy 3:23-27 and Deuteronomy 34:4-6 for the detailed account. No matter the number of baskets you use to cover smoke, it may only take some time, it will definitely find its way out, and by that time it would have become a thick smoke, uncontrollable.

Before we go any further, it is important we clearly state here that your character is not the same as your reputation, so that you will not be deceiving yourself. Your reputation has to do with peoples' comments or view about you. That is what people say you are or see you to be - which can be true or false. But your character is who you really are - in and out. Bill Hybels wrote a book and titled it

"Who you are when no one is looking". That is it, you are that person you are when you are not being watched.

Take for instance, people hail you here and there, singing your praises; saying you are a God-sent philanthropist. You donate generously to motherless babies' homes, orthopedic hospitals, charity organizations; as a matter of fact, people see you as the "Jesus of this century". But deep down within you, you know fully well that you are a thief, a cheat and a fraud at the same time. In fact, it is part of the money you steal from the people that you give back to them in the name of charity. You are a bad tree. Your character is labelled as "Thief" – that is your true self while your reputation is labelled as "A Philanthropist" - your false self. Do you understand that?

So, don't deceive yourself by being carried away by peoples' praises or reports (either positive or negative), rather focus on your character and ask yourself sincerely -"who am I?" Jacob was very sincere when asked who he was, he said "although people see me as a glorious descendant of Abraham and Isaac, full of promises and inheritance, I am a cheat, a supplanter - my name is Jacob. Little wonder his name was changed to Israel - God's own nation. His character was healed and his reputation was substantiated (Gen. 32:27-28, emphasis mine).

HOW CAN I KNOW MY CHARACTER?

This is a question I expect anyone who is interested in becoming somebody in life to ask. Someone who is ready for the top and also willing to stay there; because character does not only determine whether you climb great heights or not, it also determines whether you're staying there or coming down.

I will like to give a dual approach to answering this question. First, how you can know yourself and second, how you can know others.

- **Knowing Yourself**

The first step in knowing yourself is agreeing that you don't know yourself, and that you will like to know yourself. Take a time out and ask yourself many self-revealing questions with more emphasis on **MOTIVES**. Take a sheet of paper with your pen and answer the following questions **SINCERELY**, make sure you are alone and not under the influence of radio, television, computer system or any of such. Isolate yourself for what I call **"Self-Pouring Investigation Exercise" (SPIE)**. These are the questions;

1. What is your name and how old are you?
2. What is your temperament like? Sanguine, Choleric, Melancholy, Phlegmatic or combination of two or more of them?
3. What gives you joy the most?
4. What makes you sad or bitter easily?
5. When you were growing up, when was your best moment? And why did you give that answer?
6. Did you grow up with your parents or guardian?
7. Were you maltreated or abused early in life?
8. Have you been maltreated or abused lately?
9. What kind of offence will you never be able to forgive?
10. Do you feel loved or rejected?
11. How can you be loved? That is, what makes you feel loved?
12. Do you talk less and listen more? Or do you talk more and listen less?
13. How would you describe your relationship with the opposite sex?
14. What is your favorite movie, and why?
15. What is your best game or sport, and why?
16. What is your best food, and why?
17. Who is your best friend, and why?

18. What is your aim, goal or ambition in life, and why?
19. What do you spend your time, money, energy and strengths on without feeling tired? What takes your time and money mostly?
20. Why did you give the answers you have given so far? Go over the answers again and state your reasons.

Friends, these are not all the questions you need to answer in order to find out who you are. They are just psychological guides. The best ways I will recommend are that, firstly, you ask your Maker to show you who you really are, because He made you - Psalm 139:13. Secondly, having the answers to these questions in mind, begin to watch these things - "What you say", "What you do", "Why you say what you say" and "Why you do what you do". It is not an overnight discovery. It takes time. But you can trust the Holy Spirit to help you discover who you really are because Jesus said He would teach us all things - John 16:13.

Take for instance, you've always thought you could never cheat in an examination hall, and that has been a settled matter in your heart. So, on a particular day you find yourself in an examination hall and you've prepared well for the examination, so you are so sure of what to write. But suddenly, you forget a very simple formula which will allow you solve the compulsory question carrying 40 marks out of 60 marks. You try as much as you can to remember but to no avail. Then, suddenly, your eyes involuntarily travels to your neighbour's answer sheet and you discover he's almost through with the compulsory question and you consciously or unconsciously ask him for the formula or just glance up to see the formula and you start solving the questions.

You've just cheated and that is the real you. It therefore means, you've not been cheating all these while because you had no occasion to cheat, but the day the need arose, you cheated. That's you. It is what you see yourself do or say most times that expressly tells who you really are. The Bible confirms this in Luke 6:45. Here it says

"A good man out of the good treasure of his heart brings forth good; and an evil man out of the evil treasure of his heart brings forth evil. For out of the abundance of the heart his mouth speaks".

Your words reveal your thoughts and your thoughts show who you are. As a man thinks, so he is - Prov. 23:7.

So, what are you saying and what are you doing?

Your honest and sincere answer shows your true person.

Note this; sincerity with yourself is the key.

- **Knowing Others**

A comprehensive and clear understanding of "knowing yourself" will make knowing others easy. Once you know who you are - your true person, knowing others will not be difficult. The Bible says in Matthew 7:20 that by their fruits, you will know them.

To make it simpler, two different trees may look alike in their stem structure, branches, leaves, height, girth etc but their fruits will tell of which kind they are.

For instance, looking at banana and plantain trees; they so much look alike, to the extent that they can be confused for each other. But by looking at their fruits, one will undoubtedly discover which one is banana and which one is plantain. The fruit is what distinguishes; not the leaves or the branches. The Bible didn't say by their leaves you will know them but by their fruits. Luke 6:44a says *"For every tree is known by its own fruit"*. That is, to know a pawpaw tree, find out from the fruit, to know an orange tree, find out from the fruit, to know a mango tree, find out from the fruit and in the same manner, to know the kind of person somebody is, find out from their fruits (what they do or say). A man can pretend in works but not in fruits. A man can be sweeping the floor of the church, cleaning the chairs, writing tracts, taking praise and worship, evangelizing, carrying the Pastor's Bible, preaching on the pulpit, healing the sick, paying his tithe, giving alms and offerings, casting out demons and even raising the dead among many other miracles - **they are just "works", not fruits** (Matt 7:22-23).

The fruits consist in what he does in his closet when the Pastor is not around; his reaction towards paying of tithe, his reason for coming to church - maybe so that they will not ask after him at the end of the service; his reasons for sweeping and cleaning - maybe to possess a commitment testimony with the members of his church; his reaction when insulted, his response when disciplined, his testimony in his neighbourhood, the kind of music he listens to, his prayer life at home (not in church) among others.

Can you see how deceptive works can be, not even to the observer only, but also to the bearer? Little wonder Jesus did not say "by their works you will know them but by their fruits" - real self. So, you can know people by their fruits - what they manifest especially as a way of life. A goat cannot produce sheep. They are what they produce and you are what you produce.

~ CHAPTER FIVE ~

PRODUCING GOOD FRUITS

"Either make the tree good and its fruit good, or else make the tree bad and its fruit bad; for a tree is known by its fruit - Matthew 12:33.

The Easy to Read version puts the text above this way; *"If you want good fruit, you must make the tree good. If your tree is not good then it will have bad fruit. A tree is known by the kind of fruit it makes."*

From this text, it is evidently clear that **fruit production is a function of the state of the parent tree**. That is, a good parent tree has no choice other than to produce good fruits while a bad parent tree will inevitably produce bad fruits. The same Matthew Chapter 12 says in verse 35 that *"A good man out of the good treasure of his heart brings forth good things, and an evil man out of the evil treasure brings forth evil things"*. This clearly shows that as it is with the trees, so it is with men. And it has already been established earlier on in this book that men are like trees, bearing character as fruits.

WHAT ARE GOOD FRUITS?

In answering this question from God's perspective, Galatians 5:22-23 would be of help. It reads:

"But the fruit of the spirit is love, joy, peace, longsuffering, kindness, goodness, faithfulness, gentleness, self-control. Against such there is no law".

These are the attributes, qualities, and character traits God refers to as GOOD FRUITS. He said there is no law, neither in heaven nor on earth that can say these things are wrong. They are perfectly good.

However, to understand the nature of these good fruits very well; you would notice that "fruit" was used in the singular form, representing nine different attributes; it is because they all belong to a category as earlier said. They are like members of a family bearing a single surname.

Now let us consider the fruit briefly;

1. **Love:** Another name for this is God. 1 John 4:8 says God is love. This means for a person to manifest love, he or she will have to completely manifest God.

    You may say "that's simple, I fall in love easily". Unfortunately, that's not what I'm saying; in this kind of love, you don't fall; you stand. To be sure you have this love; write the tests in I Corinthians 13:1-8. If you possess everything listed there, you have love, but if just one is missing in your life, love is not yet a fruit in your life.

2. **Joy:** This particular fruit is inwardly generated unlike happiness which is externally stimulated. You can't be happy without a reason, but you can be joyful without any reason. It just springs forth from within you and it releases strength (Nehemiah 8:10b), hope (Romans 12:12) and Revelations (Isaiah 12:3) into your spirit man. You may not have any money left in your purse, no food in the house, no house rent, no job, no wife, no child, nothing to make you glad, yet you are singing praises to God from the depth of your heart. That is joy. However, the only place you can

experience such level of joy is in God's Presence. Psalm 16:11 says in your presence is fullness of joy. And one other thing about it is that it comes through knowledge (not reasons). It takes a "knowing" to be joyful. For instance, James 1:2-3 says "My brethren, count it all joy when you fall into various trials. Knowing that the testing of your faith produces patience". Also, Hebrew 12:2 says *"looking unto Jesus, the author and finisher of our faith, who for the joy that was set before Him endured the cross, despising the shame and has sat down at the right hand of the throne of God."* In addition to these, Psalm 30:5b says *"weeping may endure for a night, but joy comes in the morning."* So from all these, we can infer that it is the knowledge of the aftermath of a problem that keeps a man joyful even in the midst of the problem, knowing fully well that God is not wicked and that He has great plans for him. Jeremiah 29:11, I Corinthians 10:13, Romans 8:18, Isaiah 43:1-2, 49:14-16, Psalm 119:71, Job 23:10, Habakkuk 3:17-19 among others are the kinds of knowledge you need to be able to successfully exhibit this fruit called joy. Search the scriptures for more so that your joy may be full.

3. **Peace:** This fruit is synonymous to calmness, quietness, stillness and tranquility. It is a state of rest even in the midst of troubles, problems, tribulations etc. It cannot be exhibited unless there is a storm or a war. So, it does not depict the absence of problems, wars, storms, calamities etc in a man's life, it only means the fellow will still be at rest despite his situations. Can't you see this fruit is beyond normal human understanding? No wonder the Bible describes it in Philippians 4:7 as the peace of God which surpasses all understanding. However, this fruit cannot be experienced or exhibited without the consent and permission of the Prince in charge of it. His name is Jesus Christ.

You must have a relationship with Him because He alone is the custodian of peace; and He dictates when it is experienced and exhibited or not. Isaiah 9:6 confirms this. To be sure it is only the Prince of peace who can give peace, read Mark 4:35-41 and John 14:27.

4. **Longsuffering:** This is another expression for patience. It is the ability to accept delay, annoyance or suffering without complaining. It is also a fruit that has fulfilment of Gods promises as seeds. You cannot obtain God's promises without this fruit and you cannot be complete, mature and perfect without it. James 1:4 says we should let patience have its perfect work, that we may be perfect, and complete, lacking nothing. Also, Hebrews 12:1 tells us that this Christianity race which will terminate in heaven needs a great deal of patience (endurance, longsuffering). This fruit is the passport or ticket needed in journeying to the promise land. Abraham waited patiently on God for 25 years before he could receive his Isaac. This fruit comes by training and not by laying of hands. You consciously learn to trust in God (for His promises) and wait on Him even when all the surrounding factors are saying "It's too late"; "it's no more possible" etc. without murmuring, complaining or grumbling. It takes only the grace of God to manifest this fruit. For instance, Job had to wait till the 42nd chapter of his life before he was restored, and in all his ordeals, he never cursed God. Do you have this?

5. **Kindness:** This fruit has to do with showing concern or care about the happiness and feelings of others in gentle and friendly way. It is not doing to others what you will not like them do to you. Caring for people's welfare, always thinking of how someone's life can be better, feeling for others and not just showing sympathy but empathy, thinking less about your own needs so as to get others' needs

met, being merciful and compassionate, not using your authority over someone to punish them but always willing to forgive, being ready to go hungry for others to be fed, being considerate in decision making so as not to adversely affect others and so on. Simply put; kindness is all about "being like Jesus to people". He is the One who died for us while we were yet sinners - Romans 5:8, and according to Psalm 103:3 and 10 He forgives all our iniquities, heals all our diseases, He has not dealt with us according to our sins, nor punished us according to our iniquities. It is a fruit one must possess to be called a Christian.

6. **Goodness:** As the name implies, this fruit is all about being good and doing good; not occasionally, but all the time. It finds application in not rewarding evil for evil and praying for one's enemies. In Matthew 5:44, Jesus said *"But I say to you, love your enemies, bless those who curse you, do good to those who hate you, and pray for those who spitefully use you and persecute you"*. That is goodness. If you do good only to those who do good to you, what special thing have you done, do not even the sinners do so? (Verses 46-47). It is paying good for evil that makes you a bearer of goodness and not just being good to your family members, friends, church members etc. Verse 45 tells of God's own goodness. It says He makes His sun to rise on the evil and on the good, and sends rain on the just and on the unjust. Did you see that? Have you ever wondered why people who kill for money rituals, witches, wizards, herbalists, prostitutes, liars, thieves, armed robbers, kidnappers, terrorists and even you still celebrate birthdays - numbering years? It is because of God's goodness. To Him, all weeds are potential roses. He doesn't look at our evil sides, rather He looks at what we can still become by virtue of His investments in us. To possess this fruit therefore, you must train your

mind and learn to see only the good things in others, (not their faults).

7. **Faithfulness:** This fruit is best expressed as an unalloyed, unwavering, unflagging, unfettered, unfeigned, unfathomable and unflinching loyalty to a person or a cause. It is believing in somebody or something and willing to die for it. As Christians, faithfulness should not only be demonstrated when all our prayers are being answered. It is more needed when things are not moving smoothly. Somebody said "When faithfulness is most difficult, that's when it's most necessary". The best time to show forth this fruit is when it logically makes no sense to do so. A very good example of those who exhibited this fruit are the three Hebrew boys in Daniel 3:1-30. Please try and read the whole story. Shadrach, Meshach, and Abed-Nego said something awesome in verse 17 - 18 when being threatened to be thrown into the fiery furnace. They said *"If that is the case, our God whom we serve is able to deliver us form the burning fiery furnace, and He will deliver us from your hand, O king. But if not, let it be known to you, O king that we do not serve your gods, nor will we worship the gold image which you have set up"*. That was a dangerous statement in the presence of a king; but a challenge in the presence of the King of kings. What they were saying in essence is that "Even if God fails us in this matter; even if His promise of protection does not come to pass; even if we are put to shame defending Him; even if everyone laughs us to scorn because of Him, saying we are stupid; even if He decides to stop answering our prayers, doing miracles for us and healing our sicknesses - We know HE IS STILL GOD and we will not deny Him. We will not worship any other god; He is always God". That is faithfulness! Job said even though He slay me, yet will I trust in Him (Job 13:15) and Esther said If I per-

ish, I perish (Esther 4:16). These are statements borne out of faithfulness. You must be willing to die for what you believe in. If you trust God with all your life, you will not say "I'm not a Christian" when troubles come. God is faithful, even in our unfaithfulness (2 Timothy 2:13) and He doesn't expect anything less. In addition to this, faithfulness is a fruit expected to be manifested in our day to day activities, especially in our commitments - job, work, career, profession, academics, contracts, payment of house rent and utility bills, farming, trading etc. It is doing things right, even when not being monitored or supervised. For instance, if resumption time is 8am in your place of work, you are expected to resume at that time not only when your boss is around but always (whether he is around or not). Faithful people don't do things the way it is being done but, the way it should be done. Without this fruit, you will never leave your present level according to Matthew 24:45-47 and 25:14-30.

8. **Gentleness:** This fruit has to do with being mild, careful, harmless, not rough or violent etc. It is having a dove-like spirit. A bearer of this fruit does not harm anyone, - not in deed, actions, words, reactions, conducts, or even in thoughts. It is living an easy-going lifestyle. A person with this fruit can be referred to as a lamb or sheep. They don't argue with instructions, they don't give excuses, they don't use harsh words, they are not lousy or loquacious, they are cool headed. In fact, this fruit makes people see them as stupid and foolish because they don't claim and fight for their rights, they keep quiet when cheated; they are not violence conscious students; they always leave everything to God; and God in turn defends them. Just as a sheep cannot survive without the shepherd, the gentle cannot do without God. They have put their complete trust in Him,

and that's why they don't bother themselves. They know whatsoever you do to them, you have done to God - either positively or negatively so they just hold their peace. The moment you possess this fruit, you will begin to be seen as a dangerous, untouchable Christian. But if you are still defending yourself, meekness is far away from you and you will keep struggling with offenders. To be gentle, become humble like the earth (i.e. the ground that takes all insults without complaining).

9. **Self-Control:** This fruit is otherwise referred to as temperance; and it is the ability to control one's behaviour or not to show one's feelings. It is not a once in a while thing, but a practice. It involves consciously restraining oneself in many ways. This is a fruit you must compulsorily bear if making Heaven is still your goal. And not only that, if you don't want to die a nonentity; but a greatly fulfilled person, you must not joke with this fruit. The Bible did not just say "control" but "self-control". It is therefore your job not God's, although you still need His grace. Proverbs 16:32b says *"And he who rules his spirit than he who takes a city"*. That means conquering a whole city is no big deal at all when compared to controlling oneself. Self-control is a fruit needed in not just an area of one's life but in every area. For instance, it is needed in eating and drinking (what, when and where to eat and drink), dressing, sleeping, talking (the most difficult), spending (of money, time, energy, interest etc), thinking, looking, hearing, anger, loving, reading, laughing, smiling, relaxing, traveling, pleasure, rejoicing, praying (aloud or quiet), dancing, playing, liberty, conviction, prophecy; in fact, in all the things you say and do while you are still living. You would notice some honourable things like prophecy, praying, rejoicing, conviction etc were included in the list. Yes, they are noble and

good but only in moderate proportions. When in excess or uncontrolled, they can easily become sins. Philippians 4:5 says "Let your moderation be known to all men. The Lord is at hand". And Apostle Paul also said in I Corinthians 9:27 that he disciplined his body and brought it into subjection, lest when he had preached to others, He himself should become disqualified (or be cast away). That is self-control. To make it simpler, self-control is also about saying 'No' to what your flesh wants you to do; it means not responding to the dictates of the flesh. Obviously, we know the flesh only drives us towards death according to Romans 8:6; and that the spirit is what gives life. Good! So, we are constantly in the battle of who to please, the flesh or the spirit because they are direct enemies (Galatians 5:17). And it is an already established fact that those who are in the flesh cannot please God (Rom 8:8). How then can you possess this fruit of self-control? Very simple. Walk in the Spirit. Galatians 5:16 says "I say then: walk in the spirit, and you shall not fulfill the lust of the flesh". That's the only way out. Remember, self-control is a fruit of the Spirit and not of your wisdom or power. So, you will need the Spirit to bear it, even though the constant practice is yours to do. For instance, in controlling your tongue, no New Year resolution will ever be able to help you because James 3:8 says *"...no man can tame the tongue. It is an unruly evil, full of deadly poison"*. This fruit called self-control can only be exhibited in partnership with the Holy Spirit, just like other fruits earlier mentioned.

Having considered what these good fruits are - their attractiveness and their beauty, it is worth noting that they can't jump on any man. They must be borne. Jesus Christ said in that Matthew 12:33 that for a fruit to be good, the tree bearing it would have to be made good (paraphrased). All the aforementioned fruits are called "The fruit of the Spirit"; and there is only one person in charge of them. His name is Jesus Christ.

While He was on earth, he exhibited all of them without failing in even one – Hebrews 4:15. The next verse says *"Let us therefore come boldly to the throne of grace, that we may obtain mercy and find grace to help in time of need"*. What this is saying in essence is that "seeing the need to possess these fruits and knowing fully well that our trees (nature) are not naturally configured to bear them due to the wrong fruit our father Adam ate long time ago, we can now apply Jesus Christ as a 'FERTILIZER' to our own tree so that it can yield the desired fruits". And to get this free 'Fertilizer', we will have to visit the throne of grace where it is being distributed". That is it.

You can't bear Jesus' fruits without applying Jesus. So if you are interested in applying Him for good fruits yield, say these as a prayer". **Lord Jesus, I thank you for granting me access to the throne of grace this hour. I acknowledge my sins and I ask for your mercy this moment. Have mercy on me, cleanse me in your blood, wash away my wrong fruits and write my name in the Book of Life. I open the door of my heart to you in response to your knock. Come into my life and be my personal Lord and Saviour. Help me to start bearing your own kind of fruits and don't let me stop bearing them till I see you in glory. Thanks for saving me, Amen.** You can now start producing "Good Fruits" because your tree has just been made good (Matthew 12:33). Praise God!

~ CHAPTER SIX ~

REMAINING A GOOD TREE

"*Whoever has been born of God does not sin, for His seed remains in him; and he cannot sin, because he has been born of God*". I John 3:9.

The Living Bible Translation puts this verse this way; **"The person who has been born into God's family does not make a practice of sinning, because now God's life is in him; so he can't keep on sinning for this new life has been born into him and controls him - he has been born again".**

"*they shall still bear fruit in old age; they shall be fresh and flourishing*"

"*whoever has been born of God does not sin, for His seed remains in him; and he cannot sin, because he has been born of God*" "*His seed remains in him; and he cannot sin*" "*...Ye are gods...*" "*So God created man in His own image ...*"

It therefore follows that to remain a good tree (as a god), you must continue to behave like the Parent Good Tree (God), just like a goat must not be found behaving like a cat or a dog. Whatever God will not do must not be found in your way of life because you carry His seed. For instance, God does not practice any of the works of the flesh listed in Galatians 5:19-21 as adultery, fornication, uncleanness, licentiousness, idolatry, sorcery hatred, contentions, jealousies, outburst of wrath, selfish ambitions, dissensions, heresies, envy, murders, drunkenness, revelries, and the like. (I would recommend you take a dictionary and get the meanings of these works). If any of them is found in your life, you have lost this seed and like the prodigal son, quickly arise and come back to your Father by crying to Him for mercy. Don't ever justify any appearance of evil or sin in your life. Don't wait until you are sure it is a sin; once you discover it looks like sin (1Thessalonians 5:22); quickly cry to Him for forgiveness and he will in turn give you His peace as a sign of restoration. In addition to this, constantly fellowship with believers (not church goers or bench warmers but saved souls) in any Bible believing church where Jesus is being honoured and recognized as the Lord. It will assist God's seed in you to grow faster, yielding more fruits unto righteousness.

Pray always, giving thanks and asking God for help all the time because the devil your adversary is not taking it easy at all; he wants you back in his kingdom of darkness; but he will fail in your case. Amen. Although 1 Peter 5:8 says he is like a roaring lion seeking whom he may devour, it is very important to know that he is only "like" it, he is not a lion and he can never be; because there is only one Lion and that is the Lion of the tribe of Judah. So, that is taken care of. More to this, guard your windows - what you hear, see, smell, taste and even think in your heart must be pure and noble - Philippians 4:8. Defilement comes easily. Don't also allow the worries of this life to take you back to Egypt. Focus your attention on Jesus, the Good Shepherd; and all your needs will be supplied - (Psalm. 23:1, Philippians 4:19, 1 Peter 5:7, Matthew 6:25-34 among other Scriptures contain His promises of provision). Finally, feast regularly on the Word of God. The Word of God is Jesus Christ and feeding on Him is what guarantees remaining a good tree (John 1:1-4; 14). Psalm 119:9 says *"How can a young man cleanse his way? By taking heed according to Your word".* Verse 11 of the same chapter says *"Your word I have hidden in my heart, that I might not sin against You."* It didn't stop there, John 15:4-5 says *"Abide in me, and I in you.*

As the branch cannot bear fruit of itself, unless it abides in the vine, neither can you, unless you abide in me. I am the Vine, you are the branches. He who abides in me, and I in him bears much fruit, FOR WITHOUT ME, YOU CAN DO NOTHING." That is the declaration of the WORD Himself. So, get a complete Bible, not just New Testament, but a full one and start feasting voraciously on it. If God sees your seriousness as you thirst and hunger for His knowledge, He will fill you, and once He does, bearing good fruits becomes a natural sequence.

~ CHAPTER SEVEN ~

THE DANGER OF UNFRUITFULNESS

The danger of unfruitfulness is WITHDRAWAL, leading to DESTRUCTION – an irreversible type. Let us not talk too much, the Bible states it clearly.

- *John 15:2, 7 - "Every branch in me that does not bear fruit He takes away.... He is cast out as a branch and is withered, and they gather them and throw them into the fire, and they are burned."*
- *Mark 11:12-14, 20 - "...He was hungry. And seeing from afar a fig tree having leaves, He went to see if perhaps He would find something on it. And when He came to it, He found nothing but leaves, for it was not the season for figs. In response Jesus said to it, "Let no one eat fruit from you ever again". ...Now in the morning as they passed by, they saw the fig tree dried up from the roots".*
- *Matthew 25:24-30 - "...But his Lord answered and said to him, You wicked and lazy servant, you knew that I reap where I have not sown, and gather where I have not scattered seed. Therefore, you ought to have deposited my money with the bankers, and at my coming I would have received*

back my own with interest. Therefore, take the talent from him... And cast the unprofitable servant into the outer darkness. There will be weeping and gnashing of teeth".

These are just to mention a few; but you would notice that in each case, there was firstly a withdrawal before the pronouncement of destruction. He first takes away the unused ability to bear fruit (and most times gives it to effective fruit bearers) before finally destroying the fellow.

In the second instance, the Bible says the fig tree had no fruit because it wasn't its season, yet Jesus cursed it. This tells us something expressly, "There can never be any legitimate reason for unfruitfulness". No excuse no matter how genuine can be accommodated by your Master. Fruit bearing is compulsory as long as His seed (life) remains in you. Deuteronomy 7:14 says there shall not be a male or female barren among you or among your livestock. "There shall not be" here means "it will not exist". Instead of it to exist, He says I will rather take such a fellow away before he disgraces the efficacy of My word. You can't afford to be unfruitful. Try and check your life, if there is a particular thing you were capable of doing before, something you were good at or a major trait or behaviour you were once described with and it looks as if it's no more in your life; withdrawal is likely to have taken place, and if you don't cry for mercy urgently, destruction may set in. I pray the Lord will not destroy you in Jesus' name. And because He is the God of a second chance, He will restore His withdrawn grace back to you. However, this may be your last chance; bear fruits to glorify Him (Luke 13:6-9).

~ CHAPTER EIGHT ~

THE DANGER OF BEARING BAD FRUITS

The danger of bearing bad fruits is very much similar to that of not bearing fruits at all; only that a process is involved in this case.

Let us look at it clearly from the scriptures; Isaiah 5:1-7:

"Now let me sing to my well-beloved, a song of my beloved regarding His vineyard: my well beloved has a vineyard on a very fruitful hill. He dug it up and cleared out its stones, and planted it with the choicest vine. He built a tower in its midst, and also made a winepress in it; so He expected it to bring forth good grapes, but it brought forth wild grapes. And now, O inhabitants of Jerusalem and men of Judah, judge, please, between me and my vineyard.

What more could have been done to my vineyard that I have not done in it? Why then, when I expected it to bring forth good grapes, did it bring forth wild grapes?

And now, please let me tell you what I will do to my vineyard: I will take away its hedge, and it shall be burned; and break down its wall, and it shall be trampled down. "I will lay it waste; it shall not be pruned or dug, but there shall come up briers and thorns. I will also command the clouds that they rain no rain on it.

For the vineyard of the Lord of hosts is the house of Israel, and the men of Judah are His pleasant plant. He looked for justice, but behold oppression, for righteousness but behold weeping".

That was God's declaration concerning His chosen people, Israel and of course His declaration for this present generation of His redeemed people since He is the "I AM THAT I AM" Who changes not. So, don't console yourself by saying: "That was in the old testament".

Like in the previous chapter, the danger of bearing bad fruits is also WITHDRAWAL, leading to DESTRUCTION, but in between these is a stage called DEGENERATION PROCESS. That's the difference. In the case of unfruitfulness, destruction is instant after withdrawal of grace. But in this case, after withdrawal of grace, the fellow will suffer disgrace for a period of time (degenerating in the process) before he is finally destroyed. It is like a dilemma, none of them is good because they both lead to destruction.

According to that passage, God said He would withdraw His support, grace, coverage, protection, provision etc and cause the bad tree (producing bad fruits) to experience what it looks like to be without them for a period of time before finally destroying it (Luke 3:9). This is a dangerous one; may God have mercy on us.

Examples of people who fell into this category in the Bible are:

1. **King Saul:** He was anointed as king over God's precious heritage; and all God was expecting from him was constant and absolute obedience. But he yielded a very bad and sour grape called disobedience. And as a result he lost his kingdom, another king was anointed while he was still alive, he started misbehaving by reason of the evil spirit that came upon him from the Lord, he started consulting the dead, he was really tormented and at the end, the Bible says he died as if he was never anointed (1 Samuel 10; 15; 16:14; 28:3-20; 31:1-13 and 2 Sam 1:21-27).

2. **Adam and Eve:** They lost their place with God due to disobedience (a bad fruit) and they toiled, suffered and travailed (without grace) till they died (Genesis 3:1-24, 5:1-5).
3. **Samson:** He was heavily anointed, right from the womb of his mother. But he brought forth a bad grape, which was an uncontrolled appetite for sex with strange women. He lost his place with God and made sport for his enemies right in their midst with his eyes plucked out before he finally got destroyed with the enemies he was created and anointed to destroy (Judges 13:5-25; 16:1-31).
4. **Eli:** He was a much respected priest of God with high level of anointing. But at some points in his life time, he manifested a very bad grape called "indifference" towards the nefarious attitude of his children. He could not control them despite the harm they were doing towards God's heritage. God then stopped speaking to him and he lived the rest of his life a deaf and blind Prophet. His oil dried up in his very lifetime and he was replaced by a very small boy staying under his own roof. And to make the matter worse, God prophesied his doom through the small boy and his two sons died on the same day while he himself fell from his chair and died a shameful death, because that's not the best way for a prophet to die. He also incurred an everlasting curse for his descendants (1 Samuel 2:12-17, 22-36; 4:11, 12-18).
5. **Moses:** He is another example. It is highly unfortunate to have Moses included on this kind of list. But that tells us that no matter our level of closeness to God; His standards are still His standards; He cannot lower them. Moses was very great. As a matter of fact, I can't start writing about his many exploits. You know what I'm talking about. Someone who spoke with God mouth to mouth. It wasn't a joke. However on a very particular day, Moses - the great, manifested

just one (not even two), but one bad fruit called anger; and he wasn't spared. He lived with regret for the rest of his life by reason of God's verdict: he was not to enter the Canaan land he had laboured for all his life. This happened when it remained just a little while to get there. He was replaced by Joshua and the Lord killed him Himself after showing him the land he would have entered. It is a fearful thing to fall into the Hands of the Lord, for who can save you from His Hand?

These are just to mention a few. It therefore becomes highly important for us to constantly check the fruits we are bearing so as to ensure they are good ones. 1 Corinthians 13:5 says ***"Examine yourselves as to whether you are in the faith. Prove yourselves. Do you not know yourselves that Jesus Christ is in you? - unless indeed you are disqualified"***. I pray as we consciously watch and take note of the fruits we are bearing, the Lord Almighty Himself will help us bear the good ones.

And may the grace of our Lord Jesus Christ, the love of God and the fellowship of the Holy Spirit be with us now and forever more. Amen.

PRAYER POINTS

- Lord Jesus, make my tree good, that I may produce good fruits.
- Father, destroy every negative fruits in my life.
- Father, every good thing I have lost by reason of my bad fruits or unfruitfulness, please mercifully restore them to me.
- Lord Jesus, turn every form of barrenness in my life to fruitfulness.
- Lord Jesus, hold me close to your embrace and cause me to see you in glory.
- Go ahead and give God praises.

BECOME A FINANCIAL PARTNER WITH JESUS

At *Global Emancipation Ministries - Calgary*, our mandate is *to liberate men through the knowledge of the Truth* and our mission statement is *creating channels through which men can encounter the Truth [Isaiah 61:1-3; John 8:32, 36; I Thessalonians 5:24].*

Our Ministerial Activities include Rural and Urban Evangelical Outreaches, Prison Evangelism, Hospital Ministrations, Mobilization for Missions Support, Teaching of the undiluted Word of God, Scripture-Based Seminars, Discipleship, Training of Field Missionaries and Empowerment of underprivileged ones among other Field Ministerial Tasks.

Please join us in these kingdom projects by making your weekly, monthly, quarterly or annual donations to Global Emancipation Ministries – Calgary.

You can visit the "GIVE" section on our website: www.gloem.org to learn about ways to give.

For acknowledgement, please advise your donations to us by email: info@gloem.org or emancipation4souls@yahoo.com, and kindly include your details i.e. name, address, email and location. Alternatively, you can simply call +1 587 9735910 to do same.

You can also volunteer your gifts and talents in the service of the Lord through our ministerial platforms regardless of your location. To get information on how to go about this, please visit www.gloem.org and contact us via email: info@gloem.org or emancipation4souls@yahoo.com.

God bless you.

ABOUT THE AUTHOR

 By the special grace of God, **Anthony O. Adefarakan** is the privileged President of **Global Emancipation Ministries - Calgary (GLOEM)** with headquarters in Canada, North America and **Emancipating Truth Ministry International (ETMI)** with headquarters in Nigeria, West Africa.

The Lord called him into the field ministry in February 2008 with the mandate to liberate men through the knowledge of the Truth, and by December 2012 he was ordained and commissioned as the Pioneer Pastor – in – Charge of The Redeemed Christian Church of God, Revelation Parish, Shalom Area under Delta Province III, Nigeria where he served until 1st February 2015 when he officially handed over to a new Pastor in order to focus on his field ministry to which the Lord had earlier called him and for which the authority of the church had already prayed and released him to undertake.

On 29th September 2013, he was awarded a Post Graduate Diploma in Tent – Making Mission from the Redeemed Christian School of Missions, Nigeria (RECSOM, Asaba Campus) where he also had the privilege to train Pastors and Missionaries as a lecturer in 2017.

Since the commissioning of his field ministry in 2015 he has had the opportunity to lead his ministry officers to field ministrations in different Prisons, Hospitals, Orphanages, Rural communities, Camp settlements, Markets, Local churches among other places with great successes on all occasions – such as salvation of sinners, healing of the sick, financial empowerment of mission churches, provision of relief materials to the poor, provision of medical services to the underprivileged, baptism in the Holy Ghost, deliverance from demonic oppression, release of inmates just to mention a few - all to the glory of God Who alone is the Doer.

He is the author of other best-selling titles such as ***Learning from the Ants, It's Your Size, The Immutability of God's Counsel, Surely there is an End, Life Applicable lessons from the Book of Ruth, The Law of Kinds, One thing is Needful , Life Applicable Revelations from God's Word*** among others.

He is happily married to Ifeoluwa A. Adefarakan and their marriage is fruitful to the glory of God.

Jesus is his Message, Freedom is the Outcome!
Isaiah 61:1-3

www.ingramcontent.com/pod-product-compliance
Lightning Source LLC
Chambersburg PA
CBHW042235090526
44589CB00001B/6